THE CHASTITUTE

A PLAY IN TWO ACTS

JOHN B. KEANE

THE MERCIER PRESS
DUBLIN and CORK

The Mercier Press Limited
4 Bridge Street, Cork
25 Lower Abbey Street, Dublin 1

© John B. Keane, 1981

ISBN 0 85342 643 0

Printed by Litho Press Co., Midleton.

The Publishers wish to acknowledge the generous assistance of the Arts Council in the publication of this play.

The scene is set as John Bosco tells his story from his own kitchen table. The table may remain throughout; we remain aware that he is recounting his story and illustrating it with scenes from his past.

All locations are suggested rather than realistic.

ACT ONE

ACT TWO

To Cecil Sheehan

ACT 1 SCENE 1

Action takes place in the large kitchen of an old farm-house in the south-west of Ireland. Night-time. Seated by a venerable Stanley range is John Bosco McLaine. He is late fiftyish, balding, decaying, sportily if badly dressed in bright tweeds. At the time he is polishing a shotgun. He drinks occasionally from a punch glass. He refills glass from a large jug on range. He puts gun aside and rises. He takes glass with him and faces audience.

JOHN: Look at me and tell me what you see. Go on. If you said I was a farmer you would be correct. That is what I am, a farmer, a bachelor farmer. It's the bachelor bit that complicates the whole business. I'll tell you the truth. What I really am is a disaster. *(Swallows from glass)* This is punch I'm drinking. It's about the only thing I'm good at, the making of punch. Of course I shouldn't be drinking it. My doctor has warned me that if I don't give it up I'll soon be growing daisies. He says the liver is going. But what am I going to do if I stop drinking? *(Swallows again)* Maybe if I had married I'd be all right now. I tried. God knows I tried. I'd still marry any decent woman between the age of thirty and the old age pension. But it's too late for that now. I muffed all my chances. *(Drinks)* You want to know why I am a disaster? You do? You don't. I'll tell you any way. In the first place my name is against me. John Bosco McLaine. It suggests a spoiled priest or a Christian Brother. It was my mother who insisted on the name. It was her contribution to the John Bosco canonisation movement. Twelve years after I was born John Giovanni Melchior Bosco was canonised a saint. My mother died happy. Her choice of name was vindicated.

5

VOICE: John Bosco. John . . . .

JOHN: That'll be the aunt calling. *(Answers)* Yes Auntie.

VOICE: Is there somebody with you?

JOHN: *(Calls back)* Nobody — more's the pity.

(To audience) We had a heart-to-heart lately, the aunt and myself. I was sitting over there, oiling my gun. *(Resumes seat by range)* I must have been talking to myself. She walked in out of the blue expecting to see somebody with me.

(Enter Aunt Jane)

JANE: *(Surprised at seeing nobody else)* Isn't there somebody with you? You've been talking to yourself again. It's that punch. That stuff is going to kill you, you know that, John, don't you?

JOHN: Nonsense.

JANE: You drink far too much John.

JOHN: Just a few glasses.

JANE: At the rate your're going you're headed for disaster. *(Ponders a moment or two)* You know John I've been meaning to talk to you for some time. Please put that gun away and sit over here to the table. *(John does as she bids but brings punch jug and glass to table)* I'll come to the point John. I wasn't going to break it to you for some time but it's better this way. I'm getting married.

JOHN: Married!

JANE: Yes John. Married. He's a widower, older than I. We like each other. God knows he's asked me often enough. Finally I said yes.

JOHN: Congratulations Aunt Jane. I'm delighted for you. I really am. Do I get to give you away?

JANE: If you keep drinking the way you are I'll have to look for somebody else.

JOHN: I'll cut it down. I promise.

JANE: What worries me is that I may not be able to come for long week-ends like I used to. You'll be alone here all of the time.

6

JOHN: I'll be alright.

JANE: Not the way you're going. I have every notion of advertising for a housekeeper.

JOHN: For me?

JANE: Who else?

JOHN: You won't get any self-respecting woman to housekeep in this place. It's too isolated.

JANE: Not for the right person. What you need is a sound sensible woman, a widow maybe, someone who knows how to look after a man. Then . . . after a while . . . you never know how things might turn out. It wouldn't be the first time a man married his housekeeper. But getting you a housekeeper is only one item on the programme.

JOHN: You mean you have other plans for me?

JANE: Frank, he's the man I plan to marry, well Frank is a man who doesn't let the grass grow under his feet. We put our heads together one night last week over a drink and you won't believe what we came up with.

JOHN: Try me.

JANE: A matchmaker.

JOHN: A matchmaker?

JANE: Yes. ·

JOHN: I don't know any matchmaker . . . Wait a minute, you're not thinking of Mickey Molly?

JANE: Why not? He's married worse-looking than you and older than you and poorer than you.

JOHN: But a matchmaker and Mickey Molly to boot?

JANE: Beggars can't be choosers John. The least you can do is meet the man and talk to him. You're not obliged to sample his wares. I've asked him to come here tonight.

JOHN: Tonight? But —

JANE: That's settled then. (Rises) Now there's another thing.

JOHN: What's that?

JANE: I've watched you a few times in the pub or at the

7

hotel in Bannabeen. You just sit there — drinking.

JOHN: What do you expect me to do?

JANE: The place is literally crawling with women. Have you tried approaching one and offering her a drink? Might soften her up. Think about it. I'll go prepare that ad.

(Exit Aunt Jane)

JOHN: *(To audience)* She doesn't know what she's talking about. The unattached women of today burn up vodka and gin as if they had jet engines inside. If it made them drunk itself, but what happens is that they become more crafty with every dollup. I've been led up the garden path a hundred times. I softened them up but it was others who reaped the harvest. It was my ground-work made them lower their defences but it was always another who slipped in for the k.o. That's the story of my life — nearly. I nearly got there a thousand times but nearly never bulled a cow. I've come close. Had a few narrow wides, even struck the crossbar but I never got the ball in the net. It's driving me crazy. Hard to believe, isn't it, in this day and age with morals at their lowest ebb, that I have yet to have a woman. *(Pours from jug to glass)* You know the two things that militated most against my endeavours with the opposite sex? I'll tell you. Number one . . . missionaries and number two. . . townies. For townies you can read city slickers or any other kind of pervert from a built-up area. *(Swallows)* In my heyday the missionaries frightened the wits out of all the likely girls and women, even widows. I remember when I had the Baby Ford I had this young thing set up for the caper. A man with his own transport was halfway towards seducing a girl in those halcyon days. Earlier that night she had attended the mission as indeed I had. There were two missionaries. This was a great gimmick entirely. You'd have the cross fellow and the quiet fellow moryah. The quiet fellow

8

was all coaxing and cajolement, never raising his voice.

(Two brown-robed missionaries appear)

GENTLE M: Dearly beloved brethren. When evil thoughts assail you in the dark of the night, in the loneliness of your bed, pray, pray for holy purity and dismiss those lascivious desires that are sent by Satan. Pray for holy purity and dwell not on thoughts of lust, . . . *(Muttering a prayer he withdraws)*

JOHN: Now we come to the cross fellow. He would rant and roar and rage and spray the first ten pews with showers of spittle.

CROSS M: You have all of you lighted a match. You have all been burned by the flame and drawn back your hand and clutched it under your arm with the pain. Imagine a pain one million times worse, a pain that sears and blisters the entire body, a pain that cannot be endured so awful is its everlasting agony. *(Raises voice slowly until he is roaring at the top of his voice)* Can you imagine this indescribable torment? Well this is what awaits every fornicator and degenerate masturbator in this church . . . *(He trembles, overcome. Exit)*

(Hymn. Faith of Our Fathers)

JOHN: See what I mean. *(Swallows)* There we were, this girl and I, sitting happily in the Baby Ford. *(We see couple in Baby Ford, their actions suiting his words)* Earlier in the fish and chip shop after the pubs shut we had sated ourselves with chips and sausages. Only one hunger remained to be filled. The Baby Ford was parked overlooking a valley a few miles from town. Picture a fine full moon and a sky studded with twinkling stars. I was thirty years of age at the time with no conquest to show for it. A better setting for seduction you couldn't ask for. *(Swallows)* I'll never forget that night. I took her hand and squeezed it gently. She responded with a

9

squeeze of her own and my heart pounded. I leaned over and kissed her. Ah she was a sweet innocent girl. Julia. That was her name, Julia. *(Swallows)* I shall never know what evil force prompted my next move. I daresay I thought it was the done thing. Without any advance notice whatsoever I suddenly thrust my hand right up under her dress. She let out an unmerciful shriek but I held on. It was do or die.

SHE: Let go.

JOHN: Never, never.

SHE: Let go or I'll report you to the missionaries. *(She runs from the car)* You ram, you dirty old ram. The vet should be got to you.

JOHN: From under her dress something had come away in my hand. I looked at it. I couldn't believe my eyes. 'Twas a rosary beads. I know. I know. I know what you're going to say. You're going to ask what was a rosary beads doing in a place like that. Sure, for God's sake, it was common practice at the time. The mothers used to stitch them to the gussets of the knickers so the daughters wouldn't surrender. The missionaries that put them up to it.

(The missionaries laugh — fade away)
(Enter Aunt Jane)

JANE: What do you think of this now John dear? *(She reads from a slip of paper)* Housekeeper wanted. Sensible woman over thirty.

JOHN: Sensible?

JANE: It's the word that's used. We don't want **any** doxies.

JOHN: Don't we?

JANE: Of course not. *(Reads)* Widow would suit. **To** cater for gentleman of . . .

JOHN: *(Swallows, shrugs)* Fifty.

JANE: In early fifties! Alright?

JOHN: Fine.

JANE: Farmer. Transport to and from church. Good plain cook. Apply box number. . .

JOHN: Sounds alright.

JANE: It's not quite right. You wish to add anything?

JOHN: No.

JANE: Have I omitted anything?

JOHN: Don't think so.

JANE: By the way John what ever happened to that nice girl I introduced to you at the nurses' dance a few years ago? What was her name?

JOHN: Dora. Dora MacMoo.

JANE: Fine girl. You seemed to hit it off with her as I recall.

JOHN: Yes. For a while yes. It just petered out.

JANE: I'll type this. I'll go over it again. I'll let you see the end result before I send it. *(To herself)* Interesting person Dora MacMoo, probably married by now. *(Exit Aunt Jane)*

JOHN: Dora MacMoo. Another muffed chance. I remember the first time I met her. It was the aunt who introduced us. I resolved to bide my time on this one. I didn't want her erupting from the back of the car like Julia. It was a lovely summer's night. *(Couple in car suit action to John's narrative)* I was seated in the car with Dora. A fine buxom girl, no shortage of anything. We were parked in a shady spot, again overlooking the river, only this time it was Cork city. The light from the street lamps was reflected in the water. I remember well three swans emerged out of the upriver reaches like faery barques. Beside me Dora sat still, breathing evenly and serenely. My heart thumped and pumped inside me till I thought 'twould burst. The minutes passed. One, then two, then five, six, seven, eight, nine, ten. I didn't want to muff my chances. I was ever mindful of Julia and the rosary beads. I bided my time. I heard her sigh beside me. After a while she sighed again and again. Then came a long, lingering sigh, more like a ullagone.

DORA: Sweet John Joseph Alaphonsus Jesus are you

dead or alive?

JOHN: With that she banged the car door in my face. I heard afterwards on good authority that she was the hottest commodity between here and San Francisco. I had muffed it again. This time I was too slow. That's the story of my life. Too slow when I should be fast, too fast when I should be slow.

(Takes a goodly swallow and replenishes glass from jug. Enter Aunt Jane)

JOHN: What now?

JANE: Will I put it in all the papers or just the local?

JOHN: Suit yourself. I still don't think it will do any good. They all want the bright lights.

JANE: Not all John. There are some who like it quiet and peaceful. I know.

JOHN: Very well. Put it in all the papers. In for a penny, in for a pound.

JANE: That's the spirit. One final, all-out assault for better or worse. Just check me out on this John. Required urgently housekeeper. Thirty to fifty.

JOHN: Make that sixty.

JANE: Very well. *(She pencils in new age)* Required urgently. Housekeeper aged thirty to sixty. To cater for single farmer, early fifties.

JOHN: Make that late forties.

JANE: Very well. *(She makes necessary adjustment)* Late forties. Excellent wages and conditions. Transport to and from church. References essential. Apply box whatever the number is. . . What do you think?

JOHN: No harm in trying.

JANE: *(Folds slip)* Please God now we'll have results. *(There is a knock at door, off)* I'll see who that is. *(Exit Aunt Jane)*

JOHN: I had ads in the papers before you know. Oh not for a housekeeper, nothing so prosaic. I advertised for the real thing. 'Respectable farmer, early forties. Owns up-to-date dwellinghouse, H. & C. and car.

R.C. Wishes to meet nice girl, twenty-five to thirty-five with view to above.' In the beginning I had results of a kind. Unfortunately they were twice the age they pretended to be. The younger girls, of course, ignore such notices. I tried again lately. 'Lonely farmer, early fifties, wishes to meet partner, middle-aged with view to matrimony.' I left it go too late. I know now with hindsight that a woman is never too old. When you're as desperate as I am there is no such thing as an old woman.

(Enter Aunt Jane followed by Mickey Molly. A week's beard adorns Mickey's face. He wears an old felt hat and long black overcoat)

JANE: You know Mickey Molly, don't you John?

JOHN: Everybody knows Mickey Molly. How are you Mickey?

MICKEY: Very well Mister McLaine thank you. Nice enough weather we're having these days.

JOHN: Not bad at all.

MICKEY: Bit of frost at night but of course that's a great sign. Frost is the boy to settle the weather. Frost, of course, is all very fine for them that's not out in it.

JOHN: Shove up to the fire Mickey. *(Mickey moves up)* Will you have a bite to eat?

MICKEY: I'm only after the supper Mister McLaine. Thanks all the same.

JANE: What about a nice cup of tea?

MICKEY: No tea for me. I'd rather chance a drop of what yourself is taking Mister McLaine.

JOHN: Of course, of course. *(Goes to range for jug)*

JANE: I'll fetch a glass.

JOHN: Sit down Mickey. *(He pours into glass which Aunt Jane has placed on table)*

MICKEY: *(Raising glass)* Here's good health to you Mister McLaine and you too Miss. *(Sits down)* I'm a busy man Mister McLaine so let's get down to cases. *(Aunt Jane sits as does John Bosco)*

JANE: As you have no doubt already guessed, Mr

13

Molly, John here wants a woman.

MICKEY: Is it a woman to marry?

JANE: Yes indeed, a woman to marry.

MICKEY: He left it go a bit late didn't he?

JANE: You mean you can't help?

MICKEY: I didn't say that Miss McLaine. What I mean is that he has the mileage up and when the mileage is up the field is cut down. It's a hard thing to have to say but facts is facts and figures is figures.

JANE: But you can help?

MICKAY: Maybe. It all depends on what he wants.

JOHN: All I ever wanted was a decent type of girl.

JANE: He doesn't want one of these modern misses, one of these so-called libbers. You know the type I mean.

MICKEY: I don't deal in that sort of dame Miss McLaine. The likes o' them cocks up their noses at the likes o' me. These modern damsels don't know rightly where they're heading. 'Tis nothing these days but booze, sex and discos.

JANE: True for you. Too true.

MICKEY: I'll tell you one thing and one thing alone about the doxies of the present time Miss McLaine.

JANE: What would that be?

MICKEY: They all wants the bull but none of 'em wants the calf.

JANE: Well now we know what John here wants. Just a plain, decent woman if that's not asking for too much.

MICKEY: Indeed it's not. I have a few good class mares that might suit. What you want Mister McLaine is a good, steady, well-bred sort of a mare that won't shy nor kick off the traces and that won't turn into a runaway.

JOHN: I wish you wouldn't refer to women as though they were beasts of burden. I simply want a wife if it's not too late in the day.

MICKEY: I know. I know. I know what you want. There

14

is first of all, however, a few questions to be asked. You may not like their tone but 'tis me that will have to face the firing squad if things don't work out in the marriage bed. When the works collapse the engineer must answer. Now Mister McLaine my lovely, decent man answer truthful and all will be well.

JOHN: Ask your questions.

MICKEY: I will. I will. *(Pauses)*

JOHN: Go on.

MICKEY: I can't. *(Glances at Aunt Jane)*

JOHN: Why can't you?

MICKEY: A lady's ears might crinkle.

JANE: I get the message.

MICKEY: Only for a few minutes Miss McLaine.

JANE: That's quite alright Mister Molly.
    (Exit Aunt Jane)

MICKEY: Your exact fancy so's I can go as near as I can to meeting your wants.

JOHN: I . . . I don't know. I'm not sure.

MICKEY: Very well. Do you want lean or thin, do you want rangy or butty . . . Would you go for grandeur or would you like them that's down to earth? Would you go for a holy Josie or a one that's forgotten the altar? Take your time now. We have the night long.

JOHN: It's . . . it's the girl herself that would matter. Her . . . her disposition. You know what I mean. Her way, her manner.

MICKEY: My lovely innocent man there is no comparing a girl's manner before marriage with her manner after marriage, as many an unfortunate man knows to his cost, but have it your way. 'Tis you'll be living with her not me. That's the purpose of these questions, to find out exactly what you want and to divide that by what we can get for you.

JOHN: Look I'd like a gentle, sincere woman who's not gone from it, someone I can get along with and be seen with.

MICKEY: I think I'm beginning to understand Mister

15

McLaine. I'm getting to have a fairly clear picture of your requirements. *(Swallows as does John. John replenishes both glasses)* Now Mister McLaine we'll start to deal with the personal stuff.

JOHN: Personal stuff?

MICKEY: Your personal accoutrements.

JOHN: My what?

MICKEY: Just answer my questions and all will be made known. Do you strip good?

JOHN: I don't follow.

MICKEY: What are you like in your pelt?

JOHN: What's the purpose of such a question?

MICKEY: In God's name man we'll get nowhere if you're to be diverting me. I'd just as soon go about my business.

JOHN: Sorry. What was the question again?

MICKEY: What are you like in your pelt?

JOHN: May I take that to mean what I am like in the nude?

MICKEY: You may indeed.

JOHN: I'm no Apollo but I'm no bag of bones either.

MICKEY: Is your belly slack?

JOHN: Slack enough.

MICKEY: Is your legs bandy?

JOHN: My legs are O.K.

MICKEY: Is your natural belongings intact?

JOHN: Natural belongings?

MICKEY: In God's name man is your undercarriage in good repair?

JOHN: Oh . . . I see.

MICKEY: Is it in good repair?

JOHN: I suppose so. But why are you asking such questions? What sort of woman would want such information?

MICKEY: It's not the woman Mister McLaine but the woman's handlers.

JOHN: Handlers?

MICKEY: Father and mother. In some cases uncle and

aunt or whoever is guardian. You see my friend some of these marrying bucks aren't all they seem to be. The father and mother will want to be sure that you're possessed of the equipment to fulfil your side of the bargain.

JOHN: This is like a bull inspection.

MICKEY: Oh no. No inspection. They'll take your word which is more than civil because there is some I know would want a doctor's cert. or a photograph. You're a man of honour. Your word will do. Many's the innocent girl, Mister McLaine, got a suck-in and found herself straddled by a man with no battery in his flashlamp. Happens all the time. Men will boast you know and women foolish enough to believe will be disappointed and deceived.

JOHN: I can get a doctor to vouch for me.

MICKEY: Your own say-so will do Mister McLaine.

JOHN: There's nothing wrong in regard to what you mention.

MICKEY: Good, good. I'm glad that's settled. It's always the trickiest part of this business. Now? Is the house clear for a woman to come in? *(Explains)* Your aunt won't be a lodger?

JOHN: No. I'll be completely alone. My aunt is getting married. I will be engaging a housekeeper, however, but naturally I would dispense with her services if I were to bring in a wife.

MICKEY: Good. Very good. You're well away I take it?

JOHN: You could say I'm moderately well off.

MICKEY: I'll leave it at that for now. Are you free tomorrow night?

JOHN: Yes.

MICKEY: Can you present yourself at the Crossroads Pub?

JOHN: Yes.

MICKEY: Alone and unaided?

JOHN: Yes.

MICKEY: At the hour of nine?

17

JOHN: Yes

MICKEY: I will introduce you then to a lady by the name of Norrie Macey. I will sit and talk with the two of you until such time as the ice is thawed. I'll leave ye to yeer own devices then.

JOHN: I'll be there. What's she like?

MICKEY: It's not what I think she's like but what you think she's like that matters. I'll bring the mare to the parade ring, it's for you to put her through her paces.

JOHN: Tell me at least if she's presentable.
(Norrie in spotlight)

MICKEY: She's a dainty bit. No one would deny that. She has a good make, she's firm and she's not excitable. *(Rises)* She has an even temper. She won't vex and she won't snap. She's a kind little mare by any reckoning. Tomorrow night. *(Moves towards exit)* Nine. *(Pauses)* Be there.
(Exit Mickey)

CURTAIN

ACT 1   SCENE 2

The following night. Action takes place at the Crossroads Bar. On a makeshift platform there is a one-man
band, drum and organ. There is a counter at opposite
end where drink is served by a barman in shirtsleeves
and a towel over his shoulder. The one-man band is
nearing the end of a waltz as John Bosco enters.

ONE-MAN: *(Stentorian)* Come along now. Come along
now. Take your partners for a tango.

*   *   *   *   *

LINK: *(John . . . in high hopes. Smartens up. Action
into Crossroads Bar, meets Norrie, who is already estab-
lished in view. Music playing. Brief scene. Norrie just
drinks and watches the goings-on, as in script. John
flounders and tries to make conversations over loud
music. Maybe he asks her to dance. She suddenly stands
up without a word and walks out on him).*

*   *   *   *   *

MICKEY: *(Joining John as Norrie exits)* How did you get
on?

JOHN: Fair

MICKEY: Fair?

JOHN: Alright I suppose.

MICKEY: You don't sound very enthusiastic. What went
wrong?

JOHN: I don't know. There was something weird about
her.

MICKEY: Weird?

JOHN: She never spoke. Just drank and watched the
goings-on around her.

MICKEY: There's many would hold with women not
talking. Did you talk yourself?

JOHN: I may have passed some remark about the
weather.

19

MICKEY: The weather has a lot to answer for. Put the weather from your mind the next time you meet her. Shove in nice and close to her and ask her does her toes be cold when she's in bed. Ask her if she sleeps heavy or light, left side or right side, on her back or her belly or maybe 'tis how she does be tossing and tumbling all night. Find out. Ply her with strong drink and nice comfortable questions of the cosy kind. Right?

JOHN: Right.

(The music starts. Enter Sylvester. During the following Sylvester picks up Juleen and they dance the tango to excess).

MICKEY: There he is, the one and only Sylvester Brady. I know him by eyesight. A regular lady-dazzler as the song says. They say that all he has to do is top the cigarette, give a flick of the eyebrows and the belle of the ball is in his arms.

JOHN: The girl is one of the McCoons, isn't she?

MICKEY: Juleen McCoon. Juleen McCoon from Tubbernaroon.

JOHN: They all say she's a flier.

MICKEY: Oh they do indeed, especially them that were never with her. As I recall however, she has been mentioned in despatches for services, you might say, above and beyond the call of normal duty. Have you approached her?

JOHN: Waste of time. Me and my equals have no chance against the likes of Brady. He's a liar and a cheat and he's landed innumerable girls into trouble — and he's a townie to boot — and still women go mad for him, at least the women around here.

MICKEY: Could this be envy?

JOHN: Envy? Him?

MICKEY: Could your dislike of him be due to his success with Juleen McCoon and all the other Juleen McCoons of the countryside?

JOHN: It's possible I suppose.

20

MICKEY: Then you'd want to change your tack my friend. Beggars can't be choosers you know.

JOHN: What's that supposed to mean?

MICKEY: It means you can't afford to be hostile towards this Sylvester Brady. He holds all the aces. There's more to be gained by joining up with him than by crossing him.

JOHN: Join up with that fellow. Never.

MICKEY: Remember Brady's in. You're out. Dang it man, buy the hoor a drink can't you. Pretend you like him even if you don't. Watch his style. Find out what it is about him that so impresses the ladies. The man is a master of his trade. Serve your time to him and you can be master too.

(They watch Sylvester as he cavorts about. The dance ends)

MICKEY: Quick. Call him over.

JOHN: I couldn't.

MICKEY: For God's sake call him. You can't afford not to. Go on man.

JOHN: *(Calls)* Eh, Mister Brady. *(John raises hand. Sylvester turns, points finger at chest to confirm that he's the one)*

MICKEY: *(Calls)* Come on over here.
(Sylvester comes to table)

MICKEY: Ah Mister Brady how are you sir? Will you join us for a taoscawn?

SYLVESTER: Alright. I'll have a drink with you.

MICKEY: What'll it be?

SYLVESTER: Remy Martin. Large.

MICKEY: A large Remy Martin! I see. What's yours John?

JOHN: Small Irish.

SYLVESTER: Bring a ginger ale will you?

MICKEY: Small Irish, large Remy Martin, ginger ale.
(Moves to bar counter)

JOHN: How's things?

SYLVESTER: Things?

JOHN: You know . . . happenings?

SYLVESTER: What sort of happenings?

JOHN: General happenings?

SYLVESTER: You mean women don't you?

JOHN: I suppose so.

SYLVESTER: Why the hell can't you say so?

JOHN: Alright. Womanwise how are things?

SYLVESTER: Can't complain. Wasn't that Norrie Macey I saw you with?

JOHN: Y. . .es.

SYLVESTER: Was it Mickey Molly fixed you up there?

JOHN: He introduced us if that's what you mean.

SYLVESTER: That's not what I mean.

JOHN: Then what do you mean?

SYLVESTER: Mickey Molly's been matchmaking for you with Norrie Macey.

JOHN: What of it?

SYLVESTER: What of it, he says? Very well. Stick to that attitude and you'll find out too late.

JOHN: Sorry. I'd like to find out now.

SYLVESTER: About this Norrie Macey. You know she's called the seven-day wonder?

JOHN: No.

SYLVESTER: How could you? Mickey Molly didn't tell you that. You want to know why she's called the seven-day wonder?

JOHN: Please.

SYLVESTER: Because she has seven children, all farmed out now, of course. A child for every day of the week.

JOHN: I didn't know she was married before.

SYLVESTER: She was married neither before nor after.

JOHN: But the children?

SILVESTER: All sired by visiting dignitaries, van salesmen, showband musicians, mobile kitchen operators, itinerant evangelists, take your pick.

JOHN: I'd never have guessed.

SYLVESTER: A liberal soul, my friend, to say the least,

22

God bless the creature. She'll marry you, of course, if that's what you want. There will be a clause, however.

JOHN: Clause?

SYLVESTER: You ask her to marry you in the morning and she'll say yes . . . yes, of course, I'll marry you but . . . I'm not going to leave down my regular clients.

JOHN: Good God!

SYLVESTER: You steer clear of Norrie Macey.

JOHN: Thanks for the tip.

SYLVESTER: That's alright. If you ever want your card marked you know where to come.

JOHN: What about the one you were dancing with?

SYLVESTER: Juleen is it?

JOHN: Well?

SYLVESTER: No tales out of school pal. Just remember one thing. Juleen McCoon carries my brand O.K.?

JOHN: O.K.

SYLVESTER: These country kittens go wild for me. I'm not boasting. I just happen to have what they want. There's no accounting for tastes.

JOHN: Don't I know. I had a half-wit who used to work for me and now he's married to a beautiful Pakistani girl in Camden Town while I can't get a woman of any kind.

SYLVESTER: What say we do something about that?

JOHN: You mean you'd help?

SYLVESTER: I said I'd mark your card didn't I? You want me to mark your card?

JOHN: Of course. Of course.

(Mickey arrives and deposits tray of drinks on table)

MICKEY: What have you two been up to?

JOHN: Sylvester promises to help me.

MICKEY: Well I'll certainly drink to that. *(All quaff)* Any immediate plans Sylvester?

SYLVESTER: Rome wasn't built in a day Mickey.

MICKEY: Rome was not Mister Brady.

SYLVESTER: *(To John)* You free on Sunday night next?

JOHN: *(Nods eagerly)* Yes.

MICKEY: For God's sake he's always free.

SYLVESTER: Can you drive me to Cork?

JOHN: Anywhere.

SYLVESTER: You're on then. I'll be out at your place by six o'clock. You bring enough money and you'll have a night to remember. I'm a little short just now so make sure you bring enough for two.

MICKEY: He'll do that. Won't you John?

JOHN: Sure, sure. That's no problem. I can collect you in Bannabeen if you like.

SYLVESTER: And have every bum in town advertising our business? Not likely.

MICKEY: He'll be ready when you call. I'll see to that.

SYLVESTER: You know Knackers' Lane in Cork?

JOHN: Just to glance at in passing. I've never sojourned there.

SYLVESTER: You know the Three Roosters public house down at the end?

JOHN: I've noticed the sign. I've never been in.

SYLVESTER: You've never been anywhere have you son?

MICKEY: That's all about to change now though.

SYLVESTER: *(Lays a hand on John's shoulder)* You might say my lad that your life is only beginning. We'll lay that bogey of yours in the Three Roosters or I'm a Dutchman. *(To Mickey)* Why didn't you tell him about Norrie Macey's pedigree?

MICKEY: Why should I?

SYLVESTER: He's your client.

MICKEY: So is she.

(Juleen McCoon appears at table)

JULEEN: They're playing our song Sylvie.

SYLVESTER: I can hear. *(The one-man band is playing a tango)* Until Sunday my friend. You're with the right mentor now. My track record is impeccable. I go back a long time. I was seduced by a sixty-year-old

24

deserted wife when I was fifteen. After that auspicious beginning I've never looked back.

(Sylvester dances off with Juleen. John Bosco comes forward for narrating. He is joined by Sylvester, Heather and a gaudy bird. On cue Sylvester steers the bird away).

CURTAIN

* * * * *

LINK: JOHN: *(Reminscing to audience)* We left for Cork in the afternoon. You can only be a success, said he, if you refuse to be diverted. You must have a one-track mind, said he, if you are to flush the bird. I honestly felt that my days as a chastitute were over. Chastitute! The word was coined by our parish priest Father Kimmerley. According to him a chastitute is a person without orders who has never lain down with a woman. He or she, as the case may be, is a rustic celibate by force of circumstance, peculiar to countrysides where the Catholic tradition of life-long sexual abstemiousness is encouraged and defended by the Catholic Church under whose strictures free-range sex is absolutely taboo. I am, therefore, a chastitute. So much for that. In the Three Roosters Sylvester procured a pair of prime doxies. He went his way with his and I went my way with mine.

* * * * *

ACT 1   SCENE 3

Action takes place in an upstairs room in a house in Cork city. Light goes up in a dingy room which contains a bed, a chair, a small table and a wardrobe. Enter a woman, thirtyish, heavily made-up, wearing a head-scarf and raincoat. She carries her shoes in her hand. Upon entering she flops on the side of the bed and takes off headscarf. She is Heather.

HEATHER: For God's sake Johnny come on. Come on. Everything's fine. We have the place to ourselves.
(Enter a tip-toeing John Bosco carrying shoes in one hand, brown paper bag of drinks in the other. He looks cautiously about)

HEATHER: See. Nobody here, just ourselves. Put the drink on the table, love. I'll get some glasses.
(Unsteadily she rises. She climbs on chair to search top of wardrobe. She fumbles around)

HEATHER: Should be here some place. *(Locates glass and hands it to John who has meanwhile placed a large bottle of Vodka and some mixers on table)*

HEATHER: You bought a full bottle, a whole full bottle of Vodka. Sylvie was right. You are a pet. *(She hands him second glass. She wobbles. She falls into his arms. They land on the bed. She kisses him. A cracked, female voice is heard off)*

VOICE: Is that you Heather? *(Silence)* Heather do you hear? Is that you?
(John jumps from bed and would be gone but Heather restrains him by holding his hand)

HEATHER: Don't panic Johnny for God's sake. It's only my mother.

JOHN: Your mother!

HEATHER: Not to worry. She's well used to this. What I mean is she's well used to visitors.

VOICE: Are you alright Heather?

HEATHER: *(Calls back)* Yes mother I'm alright. *(To*

John) Best give me a few pounds. It'll keep her quiet. *(Calls)* I'll be right in mother.

JOHN: Of course. *(He withdraws wallet, opens it and extends it).*

HEATHER: *(Leans forward to examine its contents)* I'll just take two of these. That should do it. *(Rises)* Pour a drink love. I'll be right back. Don't go away now.

(Exit a staggering Heather. John pours drink into both glasses and listens apprehensively to female voices arguing off. Enter an unkempt man wearing pyjamas. He is Heather's brother. John is shocked, frightened).

JOHN: In God's name who are you? I mean no harm. I'm innocent. Nothing has happened.

BROTHER: I'm her brother.

JOHN: Heather's brother?

BROTHER: Her brother, her only brother.

JOHN: Oh. How do you do?

BROTHER: Are you the chap Sylvie was to˝bring?

JOHN: Sylvie? You mean Sylvester. Yes I'm the man.

BROTHER: Have you any few cigarettes?

JOHN: I don't smoke.

BROTHER: You wouldn't have the price of a package would you?

JOHN: Of course. *(Willingly extracts his wallet and hands over a pound)*

BROTHER: Price of a drink?

JOHN: Sure. *(Hands over another pound)*
(Sounds of voices entering)

BROTHER: Not a word about this.

JOHN: Oh not a word.

(Brother hastily exits. Enter Heather with mother who wears nightcap and pyjamas)

HEATHER: I'm sorry about this but she insisted on meeting you. Mother this is Johnny. I invited him home for a drink.

MOTHER: *(Grand Cork accent affected)* How do you do?

27

JOHN: How do you do?

MOTHER: You're not a native of Cork are you, Mister . . .?

JOHN: McLaine. John . . . Johnny . . . Johnny McLaine. No. I'm from Kerry.

MOTHER: Kerry. I love Kerry people. Heather's father, God rest him, used to go to Kerry a lot. He was a commercial traveller you know. Most respected.

HEATHER: Mother please. Not now. *(Swallows drink in toto. Holds onto bed)*

MOTHER: He did all Kerry and Limerick.

JOHN: What line was he in?

MOTHER: Sundries.

JOHN: Sundries?

MOTHER: Zips, hooks and eyes, garter elastic, buttons, studs, moth balls, blotting paper, everything and anything. We had our own car in those days. There was not weekend we didn't go somewhere. He was a most respected man, most respected. Connected with the bishop, through his mother's people. Oh a most respected man, a daily communicant. We had a servant girl then. She was from Kerry too. Maggie something or other. My own people, of course, were connected with all the best families. My husband was most respected, oh most respected. Then one morning he went off like that! *(Clicks her fingers)* A stroke coming from the altar. Never recovered. Went straight to Heaven . . . The wreaths, the mass cards, the telegrams. How many wreaths was there Heather?

HEATHER: *(who is pouring another drink)* I forget mother. Look why don't you go to bed?

MOTHER: Very well if that's what you want. Goodnight Mister . . . Johnny. Goodnight Johnny. You must come round for tea some evening Johnny.
(Exits muttering)

JOHN: Goodnight Missus . . .

HEATHER: You mustn't take any notice of her. *(She-*

hands him his glass) Let's have a toast . . . to us. *(She clinks her glass against his. Lays her glass on table and starts to take off her coat)*

(John helps take off coat. He lays it gently across bed)

HEATHER: Don't put it there. It won't be worth tuppence.

JOHN: Sorry.

HEATHER: Put it in the wardrobe. I won't be needing it again. Do you go out with many girls?

JOHN: Not many. I haven't been out with a girl in *(Pauses)* ages.

(He opens wardrobe and hangs coat. Heather fumbles with dress)

HEATHER: Undo my back buttons will you Johnny? *(John does her bidding)* I can tell you're not used to this.

JOHN: To what?

HEATHER: To unbuttoning dresses.

(She swallows contents of her glass)

JOHN: Another drink?

(He takes glass and half fills it. Uncorks mixer bottle and adds)

HEATHER: Are you married?

JOHN: No.

HEATHER: I was engaged once. A doctor, a surgeon in the Regional. We had the date fixed, cake ordered, trousseau bought, guests invited, everything.

JOHN: What happened?

HEATHER: Died, car crash. He adored me. I could have had anybody, barristers, dentists, professors, anybody. He was the only one. I'll probably never marry now. I could be married tomorrow if I wanted. There's an army captain mad after me. He says he'll shoot himself if I don't announce the date. I've told him it's no good.

(She pulls dress over head. Speaks from beneath it)

HEATHER: I vowed I'd never do a steady line after my

29

fiancé died. He was the only one. Help me with this. Take the end and pull.

(John takes end of dress and pulls it over her head and off. Underneath she wears a slip)

HEATHER: You're the first one since he died. You really are.

JOHN: Of course.

(She sits on bed. Drains her glass)

JOHN: You want another drink?

HEATHER: *(Very drunk now)* Sure. Arthur is his name.

JOHN: Who?

HEATHER: The captain, Arthur, Arthur Dangleby. *(John adds from mixer)* He sends me flowers all the time. *(John hands her drink)* You're shy. Are you shy? Are you shy Johnny? *(John takes refuge in his glass)* Don't be shy Johnny. There's no need to be shy with me.

JOHN: Where do you work?

HEATHER: By day you mean?

JOHN: Well . . . yes.

HEATHER: The bacon factory. I'm a supervisor. I don't work there any more though. This foreman, a married man with six kids, wanted to get off with me. I'm not that kind of girl. I just couldn't stay on. Here, hold this. *(She hands him glass. She pulls slip over head and awkwardly manages to get it off. She throws it to one side. She sits on bed in bra and panties)* My hair must be a sight.

JOHN: It's lovely.

HEATHER: You're just saying that.

JOHN: No. No. I mean it. Honestly it's lovely.

HEATHER: Drink. *(John hands her the glass. She swallows last drop, allows glass to fall to floor. Head droops and she closes her eyes barely balancing herself upright with hands resting on bed. She sighs again and there is the faint rumble of a snore followed by a fitful snort or two. Then comes a full-bodied snore. She falls forward helplessly but he checks her. She*

30

*resumes former position somewhat precariously. She
snores again)*

JOHN: Heather, Heather. *(Shakes her shoulder gently)*

HEATHER: *(Opening eyes for a moment)* What? What
time is it? Where am I?

JOHN: Remember me? Johnny?

HEATHER: *(Trying to focus her eyes on him)* Johnny!
Johnny who?
*(She snores deeply and relapses into sleep. She falls
back helplessly onto bed and to profound slumber.
John stands looking at her briefly then locates his
shoes)*

JOHN: Goodnight . . . Heather.
*(There is no answer from the bed save a snore. Exit
John, tip-toeing with shoes in hand)*

CURTAIN

* * * * *

LINK: *John wonders why did he allow Heather to get
filled with booze and pass out uselessly. He took a few
days to recover from the shock and get back from Cork.
He found that in the meantime Aunt Jane had found Eva
through an advertisement and installed her. (The lights
are coming up in the kitchen on Eva.) John full of
dreams about the housekeeper, and what did he find. . .
(We see the forbidding Eva.)*

* * * * *

ACT 1   SCENE 4

Action in kitchen. A severely-dressed woman, all in
black, stands ironing clothes at kitchen table. She is the
new housekeeper Eva Kishock. Enter John followed by
Mickey Molly and Aunt Jane who is dressed for travel

and carrying large handbag. Mickey in his usual garb.
John puts his shotgun carefully to one side.

JANE: I'm away Mrs Kishock. I like to be home before
nightfall.

EVA: Very good Miss McLaine. When can we expect
you again?

JANE: Not for some time I'm afraid. There are so many
things to be seen to.

EVA: It won't be too long I hope.

JANE: Not too long. Are you quite happy here Mrs
Kishock?

EVA: Quite content thank you Miss McLaine.

JANE: You don't miss the city?

EVA: Certainly not Miss McLaine.

MICKEY: Was your late husband from the country or
the city Missus?

EVA: My late husband was a drunkard and that's all I'll
say on that subject.

MICKEY: Sorry to hear that Missus.

JANE: I'm sure you and John Bosco will get along
nicely. Well . . . Goodbye then Mrs Kishock.

EVA: Goodbye Miss McLaine.

JOHN: I'll see you to the car.

MICKEY: No, no, no need. I'll do that. You just stay
where you are and make the most of your time.
*(Mickey motions to John to make the most of his
chances with Eva. Exit Mickey and Aunt Jane)*

JOHN: *(Locates bottle and pours himself a drink)* Would
you care for a drink?

EVA: No thank you.

JOHN: I'm glad you like it here . . . You don't find it
lonely?

EVA: No.

JOHN: You don't miss the bustle of the city?

EVA: No.

JOHN: You didn't have any family did you Eva?

EVA: If you don't mind Mister McLaine it will be Mrs

32

Kishock not Eva.

JOHN: Sorry.

EVA: Nothing to be sorry about, Mister McLaine, just as long as we know where we stand. You asked if I had a family?

JOHN: It doesn't matter. It's none of my business anyway.

EVA: I had a daughter. She died when she was three.

JOHN: Sorry.

EVA: There's nothing to be sorry about. It's all over and done with. All forgotten this long time. The last thing I want Mister McLaine is for a man to be sorry for me.

(She gathers bundle of shirts)

JOHN: I'll help with those.

EVA: You what?

JOHN: Help you with . . . the . . . the clothes.

EVA: How can you help with these? There's hardly a pound weight in the lot. Knock it off Mister McLaine.

(She exits with clothes. Returns immediately to table where she returns iron to holder and folds pressing cloth)

JOHN: I'm afraid the social life around here leaves a lot to be desired.

EVA: I'm not here for the social life Mister McLaine.

JOHN: I just meant if you feel like a drink there's a pub at the crossroads.

EVA: Mister McLaine there are a few things I'd like to make clear.

JOHN: Fire away.

EVA: No offence intended but if the cap fits you know what you can do. I will not, under any circumstances whatsoever, be going for a drink with you. In fact I will not be going anywhere at any time with any man. I hope I make myself clear Mister McLaine.

JOHN: Of course. I was just . . .

EVA: I've been through this jig too many times Mister

33

McLaine and I find it's important to get the message across early. There will be no familiarity, no confidential chit-chats, no outings, no lingering pats on the posterior . . . *(John is about to protest)* Let me finish please. I'm not saying you are that kind of person Mister McLaine. I'm merely stating my position based upon past experiences. I am your housekeeper and nothing else. If I wanted the other kind of jazz I certainly wouldn't hang around here. I'm laying all this on the table now in case we should happen to get our lines crossed in future. I want to make my position crystal clear.

JOHN: Whatever you say Mrs Kishock. I was only trying to be sociable, make you feel at home.

EVA: Well it's not necessary I assure you. Just let me carry on with my job Mister McLaine and you'll have no reason to complain.

(Gathers cloth and iron and exits. John swallows some of his drink and pours another. Enter Mickey)

MICKEY: Well?

JOHN: Ice.

MICKEY: Ice is there to be thawed.

JOHN: There's no thawing this one.

MICKEY: That's a pity. She's not a bad-looking piece.

JOHN: There's a jinx on me. There has to be.

MICKEY: No there isn't. You mustn't let that night in Cork get you down.

JOHN: Cork was the biggest disaster of all. I'm a wash-out.

MICKEY: Never. Never.

(Enter Eva with some linen which she places on table. She is about to exit when Mickey forestalls her)

MICKEY: Whoa, whoa, whoa, whoa there! Whoa the blood.

EVA: Are you addressing me?

MICKEY: Yourself it is. Stand aisy awhile and pass the time with us. God's sake we're not dummies nor statues.

EVA: What exactly do you want from me?

MICKEY: Me is it? I wants nothing.

EVA: *(To John)* And you Mister McLaine?

JOHN: Nothing, nothing at all. Just trying to be sociable.

EVA: Mister McLaine please don't put me in a position where I'll be forced to give you notice. I'll cook for you, sew for you, launder for you and keep your house trim but beyond that not an inch, because you see Mister McLaine I detest men for what they're after. I loathe and despise men. Everytime I think of a man my stomach turns inside out. The only think I feel like doing to a man is spitting on him. You'll excuse me now.

(Exit Eva)

JOHN: You can feel the cold draught after her. It's as though an iceberg had passed by. She must be the coldest creature God ever made and to think it fell to my lot to have her for a housekeeper.

MICKEY: Icebergs melt, John, when the warm air circulates about them. Basically there's three kinds of women. Cold, warm and hot. Your warm woman is your best woman but there's not enough warm women to go around so we are left with the cold and the hot. The hot is all appetite and consumes too much too soon. Therefore, we must look to the cold.

JOHN: Not this one. This one won't thaw.

MICKEY: Don't be too sure. I know more about women than you ever dreamed of on a frosty night, and it's my guess there's a woman inside there somewhere and she's trying too hard to conceal it. I'll lay an acre of arable to a cowdung that this damsel can be thawed.

JOHN: Not by me. Mickey my friend at last I'm starting to see myself as others see me. The countryside is tainted by slowly withering blossoms like me. We can't be paired off or matched. We're in excess of the quota. People snigger at us. We're always good

35

for a laugh. Look at me. Over fifty years of age without raising a flag. Over half a century without a kill.

MICKEY: You're not being fair to yourself.

JOHN: You know what really knocks the sap out of a man, the one thing that really makes him cringe?

MICKEY: No.

JOHN: It's when you're my age and a woman laughs at you because you're a man. That really makes a man feel ashamed. Dirty old men they call us because we dare aspire to having women of our own.

(Enter Eva)

EVA: There is a gentleman at the back door Mister McLaine.

JOHN: Did he give a name?

EVA: He says he is Monsignor Brady.

MICKEY: That'll be the bould Sylvester.

JOHN: Show him in please Mrs Kishock.

(Eva returns the way she came)

MICKEY: The right man in the right place.

JOHN: I don't know all about that.

MICKEY: He'll get you out of yourself. Invite him to the Spring Show. A talent like his deserves an airing in our capital city. You never know what he'll land you into, and that's what counts. Anything is better than wilting away here in the hills.

(Enter Sylvester and Eva. Men exchange greetings)

EVA: Will there be anything else Mister McLaine?

JOHN: You're not retiring already?

EVA: Any objection?

JOHN: No. No. Of course not.

SILVESTER: Who is this ravishing creature?

JOHN: Sorry. This is Eva Kishock my new housekeeper. Eva . . . Mrs Kishock this is Sylvester Brady. *(They shake hands)*

SILVESTER: Housekeeper eh? Some people have all the luck. How about a sandwich?

JOHN: She's just retiring Sylvie.

EVA: It's alright Mister McLaine. What kind of

sandwich do you require?

SILVESTER: What kind of sandwich have you got?

EVA: Mutton, ham, cheese, tomato . . .

SILVESTER: A very good selection Eva. It will have to
be Eva between us, alright? Make a ham sandwich
Eva with lashings of mustard.

(Eva goes about her business)

SILVESTER: *(Calls)* Don't be long will you Eva? I'm
starving. *(Aside)* Eva, Eva I'll soon deceive ya. *(To
John)* She's a sexy bit is our Eva.

JOHN: You'd need a blow-lamp to thaw her out.

SILVESTER: No blow-lamp needed there. That's just a
façade. A defence mechanism. The right man with
the right approach, at the right time is more than a
match for the likes of your housekeeper. Are you
still interested?

JOHN: She's made it quite clear she's not interested in
me.

SILVESTER: That doesn't answer my question.

JOHN: Of course I'm interested.

MICKEY: Dang it man he's interested in anything that's
female.

SILVESTER: Alright then. Bide your time and I'll soften
her crust.

JOHN: Soften her crust indeed. With what?

SILVESTER: With the common grease of guile my
friend.

(Enter Eva)

EVA: Your sandwich Mister Brady.

SILVESTER: *(Accepts)* Sylvie's the name. Remember
that. Sylvie. And you're Eva. Join us in a cup of tea
Eva. The night is young.

EVA: I'm sure you will excuse me, Mr Brady. *(To John)*
Breakfast will be on the table at half past eight.

(Exit Eva)

JOHN: See . . . she's frozen solid boy. You'll never
come round a dame like that.

SILVESTER: And I tell you Johnny boy that beneath that

cold exterior churns the red lava of passion. She's a walking volcano. Just you be there when the gusher comes in and I promise you a crucible of lechery such as no man ever tasted. I tell you that even your bones will melt.

MICKEY: Why don't you make a jug of punch John and we'll review our strategy?

SILVESTER: And what array of blemished beauties have you lined up for him this time?

MICKEY: I have been going back over my lists those nights and 'tis only a matter of time till I turn up the right trump. *(He produces jotter and proceeds to thumb through it)* If you like I'll name a few likely mares for your approval. *(Reads painfully)* Speckles Nora, Toordrumagowna, farmer's daughter, forty, so called because the belly is speckled with freckles as was seen when she wore a bikini to her father's meadow some short years ago.

SILVESTER: Can't place her at once but go on.

MICKEY: There's a Marian Year grotto next to the house.

SILVESTER: Keep talking.

MICKEY: A stand of spruce at the left if you take the Bannaabeen road.

SILVESTER: Colour hair?

MICKEY: Black one day, brown the next.
(Sylvester shakes head)

MICKEY: She was at the farmers' social in the Bannabeen Arms last December.

SILVESTER: So was I.

MICKEY: Cast your mind back then to that occasion and ask yourself if you recall a lady as was wearing a green frock that left her bare along the entire broad of the back.

SILVESTER: I have her. A good soul in her time. Widely known for her good nature. Reformed now I daresay and anxious to settle. Too long on the road. Too long in the tooth.

MICKEY: She's not young but neither is she old.

38

SILVESTER: Sixty if she's a day. This man is deserving of better.

MICKEY: And what are we looking for? Isn't it only someone to make our beds and wet our tay and keep us company for the rest of our days with maybe a leg thrown over now and again? There's no Miss World or no Rose of Tralee goin' to make her way up here Sylvie.

SILVESTER: Point taken.

MICKEY: Lispie Suzie?

SILVESTER: Pass on.

MICKEY: What's wrong with her.

SILVESTER: Don't ask me. Ask any incapacitated soldier in the Barracks at Bannabeen. Next please?

MICKEY: *(Reads on)* Dilhooley, Daisy Crappadudeen.

SILVESTER: Sounds good. Daisy Dilhooley.

MICKEY: Oh she's as good as you'll get. As sure as there's meat in a butcher's shop this one is good.

SILVESTER: Could it be that she's too good?

MICKEY: Who's to say for certain. He won't do much better.

SILVESTER: If he wants a ready-made heir to the throne he won't do better.

MICKEY: What are you talking about?

SILVESTER: I'm talking about a slight swelling on the young lady's maw.

MICKEY: Maw?

SILVESTER: Maw, abdomen, stomach, belly. Call it what you will it won't bring down the swelling. Seven months gone I'd say. A dainty dame like that wouldn't be setting her cap for our man here if her figure was any way slack. What else have you?
(John places glasses on table having made the punch. He proceeds to fill them. Mickey thumbs through book. John takes a seat)

JOHN: Slainte.

ALL: Slainte.

SILVESTER: I declare to God this is a mighty brew.

MICKEY: He has a way with punch.

JOHN: I wish I had a way with women.

MICKEY: A man can't have a way with everything. I had a brother could castrate bonhams blindfolded yet he couldn't put a knot in his tie.

SILVESTER: Who's next?

MICKEY: Drombie Delia.

SILVESTER: Drombie Delia? Delia Drombie? Can't place her offhand.

MICKEY: A decent sort. No chicken but nice and firm. Was going for years with a man by the name of Dan Dooley. The heart gave out on Dan a few years back and he spreading manure. These past few months Delia's showing an interest in the marriage stakes again.

SILVESTER: A picture is beginning to emerge. Proceed.

MICKEY: One thing I'll guarantee and that is this. There was never a harness thrown across her since Dan Dooley died.

(He pours punch all round)

SILVESTER: What colour has she?

MICKEY: Blonde.

SILVESTER: Blonde hair?

MICKEY: Blonde hair.

SILVESTER: Age?

MICKEY: Witness can't say your honour but she's firm and she's not past it . . .

SILVESTER: Delia Drombie, blonde . . . I know her. The Lord be good to my dear departed mother. *(Crosses himself)* If she was alive today she'd be seventy-four years of age.

MICKEY: What has your mother got to do with it?

SILVESTER: Nothing except that she and Delia Drombie were in the same class at school. Next candidate please?

MICKEY: There's only one more.

SILVESTER: Last but not least eh?

MICKEY: *(Reads)* Cant, Nellie of the Tooreengarriv

Cants. A perfect lady.

SILVESTER: Nellie Cant?

MICKEY: Know her?

SILVESTER: The name has a familiar ring. Nellie Cant? Can't be sure. Know her John?

JOHN: To see. She's a Protestant isn't she?

MICKEY: All the Cants are Protestants. Would you marry a Protestant John?

JOHN: Christ Almighty man I'd marry a Mohammedan!

SILVESTER: Come on. Come on. Details.

MICKEY: Age thirty-one. A nice shy sort that never lifted her skirt unless 'twas to answer a call of nature.

JOHN: I wish you wouldn't refer to women so crudely.

SILVESTER: Why didn't she marry up to this?

MICKEY: The brother, Willie Cant *(Tips his forehead)* a small bit of a want. Spent a time you know where. All the poor bastard ever wanted was a woman, any sort of woman. So I got him a woman and now the sister is free.

SILVESTER: And you say she's a paragon.

JOHN: *(To Mickey)* That she's a good-living girl. Without shadow or stain, a good-living girl. Oh yes without doubt.

SILVESTER: Mickey — what's the catch?

MICKEY: No catch. She's a little bit odd maybe but which of us isn't I ask you? Which of us isn't?

SILVESTER: Odd?

MICKEY: A bit odd.

SILVESTER: A bit odd.

MICKEY: That's what I said.

SILVESTER: Isn't she the same Nellie Cant that thinks she's the Black Madonna?

MICKEY: Not all the time. Not all the time.

SILVESTER: Of course not, not when she thinks she's Princess Margaret. Close that damned bool and let's face up to reality. It looks like the Spring Show Johnny me lad.

MICKEY: I said it all along. The Spring Show.

41

SILVESTER: That's settled then.

JOHN: Just a minute —

SILVESTER: There's just one problem.

MICKEY: What's that?

SILVESTER: I'm a bit short of the readies just now.

MICKEY: That's no problem. John will look after that side of it. Won't you John?

JOHN: I suppose so.

SILVESTER: Good. We mustn't let the grass grow. Where's your phone.

JOHN: In the hallway.

SILVESTER: I know just the hotel. It's the ideal job for what I have in mind.
(He exits)

MICKEY: You could look happy about it.

JOHN: I know it won't work. I'm a jinx. You know that as well as I.

MICKEY: All I know is I can't help you. I seem to be out of date these past few years. As it is I'm nearly a thing of the past.

JOHN: You tried.

MICKEY: Sylvester's in touch John. You've tried it fair long enough. Time now to go foul. *(Lifts his glass)* To the Spring Show.

JOHN: *(Hesitant)* To the Spring Show.
(They lift their glasses. They clink glasses)

CURTAIN

* * * * *

LINK: *(John comes front)*.

JOHN: The Spring Show it was to be then. Another assault on the impregnable fortress of my dreams. Once more the future was bright. I hadn't a care in the world.
(The missionaries enter, smiling and nodding and wagging a finger at John)
Ah go to hell . . . I never thought of that before. I suppose some of them must end up there.

42

(He laughs. The missionaries look stern)
Sorry. I tell you what I'll do, I'll go to confession.
(The missionaries smile and exit)
That will keep them happy . . . for a while.
(John to the confessional)

(The above a suggested **LINK** into Scene 5. It helps to keep the missionaries in the action, and gives time for set change).

* * * * *

ACT 1   SCENE 5

Action takes place in the confession box of Banna-been parish church. Father Kimmerley, the parish priest, is seated centre. At either side of the box a number of old people, male and female, are seated on two stools, awaiting their turns.

JOHN: Bless me Father for I have sinned. It's three weeks since my last confession Father. I have been drunk twice since then. Well not quite drunk, half-drunk would be nearer the truth. I had occasion to use intemperate language and took the holy name of Jesus once. I nearly had intercourse with a woman. *(Kimmerley lifts his head which had been bent the better to concentrate on what he is being told)*

KIMMERLEY: I'm not quite sure I understand. You say you nearly had intercourse?

JOHN: That's right Father. I met this woman in Cork and I nearly had intercourse with her.

KIMMERLEY: Nearly. Would you elaborate my son?

JOHN: I was in her bedroom Father. She took her clothes off, . . . well some of them . . . most of them . . . and . . .

KIMMERLEY: And?

JOHN: That was all.

KIMMERLEY: Then you didn't commit any sin?

JOHN: Didn't I?

KIMMERLEY: Don't you know?

JOHN: I thought you'd tell me.

KIMMERLEY: I'm only your confessor. I cannot be your conscience. We may take it that you had no sexual intercourse as such with this woman.

JOHN: As such, no.

KIMMERLEY: Then what had you?

JOHN: Lustful designs I suppose.

KIMMERLEY: Did you place a hand on her private part?

JOHN: No.

KIMMERLEY: Any part of her?

JOHN: Well . . . at one stage I did put my hands around her.

KIMMERLEY: But you had no carnal knowledge?

JOHN: No.

KIMMERLEY: Well, what did you do?

JOHN: I've told you.

KIMMERLEY: And I don't understand.

JOHN: I went to Cork. I met this woman. We got drunk together. We went to her bedroom. She took off her clothes. She sat on the bed. I was about to take off my clothes.

KIMMERLEY: And then?

JOHN: She fell asleep.

KIMMERLEY: Then?

JOHN: I left.

KIMMERLEY: You're John Bosco McLaine aren't you?

JOHN: For God's sake keep your voice down Father.

KIMMERLEY: Don't worry. They can't hear you my son. Why do you unburden this saga of near conquest on me?

JOHN: Because you're my confessor. Because I have sinned.

KIMMERLEY: Sinned? There isn't the makings of a dacent sin in the combined doings of all the bachelors in this parish.

JOHN: I'm not talking about this parish. I'm talking about Cork.

KIMMERLEY: And I'm talking about this parish because it's my parish and you're my parishioner. You're still a chastitute. There are no marriages, no births. The young girls have gone. The boys have gone after them. You and your equals are all that's left. What am I going to say to you McLaine? Should I tell you to go forth and fornicate properly and then come back so that I can give you absolution for a worthwhile sin or should I allow you decay in your own barren chastitution — or what am I to do with you at all?

JOHN: I came here for help.

KIMMERLEY: I'm trying to help.

JOHN: It doesn't sound that way.

KIMMERLEY: I'm being cruel to be kind, man. Can't you see that? You fellows need to be jolted, to be shocked into wakefulness. Another priest might let well alone but I can't do that.

JOHN: All I want is absolution.

KIMMERLEY: It's yours with a heart and a half.

JOHN: Give it to me then and let me out of here. The crowd outside will think I'm after raping somebody.

KIMMERLEY: Never mind what the crowd outside think. You're on my conscience McLaine. I'm a down-to-earth priest. I rationalise. The Second Vatican Council should have taken parishes like this into account. Canon Law should have made special provision for the situation here where marriage is a luxury. What right have I to condemn a man who is tormented with a natural hunger for the opposite sex?

JOHN: God's sake will you keep your voice down Father.

KIMMERLEY: Sometimes I think the Catholic Church is blind to the real needs of places like Tubberganban where enforced chastity is stifling life itself. Three Hail Mary's and get out of my sight.

(John leaves the box. Comes front)

JOHN: He's a gruff old divil, Father Kimmerley, but the heart is in the right place. And he cleaned the slate. It's a light sort of feeling you get after confession. Puts the spirit back into you. I'm in form now for the Spring Show, the step is light, the mind is fresh, the soul is cleansed . . . and my imagination is saturated with the prospect of unlimited romance.

CURTAIN

* * * * *

LINK: *(Enter John, much smartened up, by his standards)*

JOHN: Here I am all dolled up and somewhere to go — the Spring Show. Me, John Bosco McLaine . . . John Bosco . . . I was telling you about my name some time ago but I didn't really finish. I'll tell you now. In a city a name means nothing, but in a country place like this a name like John Bosco Melchior McLaine can be a decided disadvantage. I want to make it clear that I am not against religion, but seriously don't you think the name reeks of sanctity, piety, and holiness? When I was ten my father died. No he didn't die, he gave up. He allowed himself to be suffocated by repeated massive doses of rosaries and novenas. After he was buried my mother dressed in black until the day she died. She'd kneel by the door where it was the draughtiest and pray for my father's soul — hours at a time, night after night. There was no need. He went straight to heaven. His hell was while he was here. I found her there one morning huddled in a little heap, stone cold. She died without a whimper. She made only two demands on her creator, my father's salvation and my virginity. Her prayers were answered on both counts. My father couldn't be any-

46

where else but heaven, and no one knows better than myself that I am a cock virgin, frustrated but intact. I'm the last of a species. A chastitute — which in simple language is the opposite of a prostitute. So have a good look at John Bosco McLaine, Chastitute, willing to break from his fetters, and headed for the Spring Show as a willing acolyte of the whoremaster Sylvester Brady.

(He is joined by Sylvester as the Spring Show scene lights up. Trudy and Suzanne also enter and take their place at a table)

*   *   *   *   *

ACT 2   SCENE 1

Action takes place at the Spring Show. Time is the afternoon. Two well-dressed, opulent-looking, early middle-aged ladies are seated at a table covered with a fringed canopy. There might be some other tables in the background. People might be seen to pass to and fro.The ladies are served by a white-coated youth who places liberally-iced drinks on table. He accepts payment for same and withdraws or collects empties from other tables. A number of advertisements might occupy the area, particularly one for Sinclair's Milking Machines. This advertisement should be the dominating feature. Enter Sylvester Brady immaculately dressed, he is followed by John Bosco who is at his brightest yet sartorially.

SILVESTER: What would you say to a drink? I'm bloody well exhausted.

JOHN: There's a bar over there.

SILVESTER: *(Looking around him shrewdly)* Let's not rush our fences. There's a likely pair.

JOHN: They look at bit stand-offish to me.

SILVESTER: They only seem like that. I'll lay odds they're the very opposite. Are you game?

JOHN: I . . . I . . . don't know what to say.

SILVESTER: Just keep your mouth shut and stick with me. *(Calls)* Bonzo, Bonzo, Come here boy. Bon-zoooooooo! *(He walks around searching for an imaginary dog. To John)* Where can he have gone to? *(He goes on all fours and looks under table. The ladies are somewhat alarmed. He lifts his hat)* I beg your pardon. It's my dog. You wouldn't by any chance have seen him would you?
(The ladies are Trudy and Suzanne. Trudy the more outgoing)

TRUDY: What sort of dog?

SILVESTER: Irish wolfhound, answering to the name of Bonzo.

TRUDY: *(Endeavouring to recall)* No, certainly not an Irish wolfhound. I'd have noticed. Suzanne?

SUZANNE: *(Shakes her head)* No.

TRUDY: Have you tried the secretary's office?

SILVESTER: Not yet. Time enough for that. *(Haloos)* Here boy, here boy. *(Takes off his hat)* I do beg your pardon. I should have introduced myself. My name is Sinclair. Sylvester Sinclair. Sinclair's Milking Machines.

TRUDY: Oh! *(Obviously impressed)*

SILVESTER: This is my friend Johnny McNab. Flew in this morning from Australia. Johnny, say hello.

TRUDY: How do you do?

JOHN: How do you do?
    (Suzanne nods)

SILVESTER: Drinks. We must have drinks.
    (He raises hand and clicks fingers loudly. Immediately the same youth appears).

SILVESTER: You see to it Johnny.

JOHN: *(To Suzanne)* What would you like?

SUZANNE: Gin please, gin and tonic.

TRUDY: Same for me.

SILVESTER: Brandy for me. Remy Martin double with ginger ale.

JOHN: And I'll have a small Irish.

YOUTH: Very good sir. *(Exit youth)*

TRUDY: Won't you sit down? *(Sylvester sits near her)*

SILVESTER: Sit down Johnny.

TRUDY: Have you got a stand?

SILVESTER: At the other end of the grounds. I'd take you there but it's so crowded. Much more pleasant here don't you think, Miss . . . eh?

TRUDY: Trudy. Please call me Trudy.

SILVESTER: Of course, of course. It will be Trudy . . . Johnny you know. *(To Suzanne)* And you are . . . ?

49

SUZANNE: Oh . . . Suzanne.

TRUDY: And you Mister McNab, are you here on business?

SILVESTER: He's on holiday. No business this time around. He lost his wife, poor fellow, just before Christmas.

TRUDY: So sorry. Suzanne and I are widows of long standing. We understand.

SILVESTER: What a coincidence.

TRUDY: And you Mister Sinclair. Are you married?

SILVESTER: Please call me Sylvie. No, my wife alas is no longer with us. Drowned two years ago, swept overboard during a cruise.

TRUDY: How terrible for you.

SILVESTER: Life must go on. Isn't that what the song says.

(Youth arrives with drinks. He deposits them on table)

YOUTH: Gin and tonic?

SUZANNE: Thank you.

YOUTH: Gin and tonic?

TRUDY: Thank you.

YOUTH: Brandy?

SILVESTER: Lay it down here boy.

YOUTH: Small Irish?

JOHN: That'll be mine thank you. *(He tenders a note)* Keep the change.

YOUTH: Thank you sir.

(Youth withdraws)

SILVESTER: *(Lifting glass)* Cheers.

TRUDY: Cheers.

(All quaff)

SILVESTER: I have the feeling we met before . . . Last Easter at Fairyhouse?

TRUDY: No.

SILVESTER: Ascot?

TRUDY: Oh dear no. I've never been to Ascot.

SILVESTER: Good Heavens, Bonzo — I'd forgotten all

50

about him . . . Trudy, why don't you and I try to locate the secretary's office and report the loss of my dog.

(John and Suzanne are obviously embarrassed)

TRUDY: What a marvellous idea.

SILVESTER: *(Standing up)* Let's bring our drinks. *(He helps Trudy to her feet and hands her the drink. Taking his own drink he takes her arm. To John)* We'll see you later.

(Sylvester and Trudy move off. There is an uneasy silence after they go)

SUZANNE: They're lucky with the weather.

JOHN: They are indeed.

SUZANNE: Are you staying in the city?

JOHN: Yes. We're booked into the Elmslands.

SUZANNE: We're just across the road, the Riversdale.

JOHN: It's a small world.

SUZANNE: Isn't it. *(Pause)* Are you really an Australian?

JOHN: No. I'm not and I didn't fly in this morning either and his wife wasn't washed overboard because he never had a wife. *(Faint romantic background music)*

SUZANNE: I guessed.

JOHN: Do you mind?

SUZANNE: No. Are you married?

JOHN: No.

SUZANNE: Ever?

JOHN: Never.

SUZANNE: How did you escape?

JOHN: Maybe I tried too hard. I wanted to . . . I just couldn't con anybody into it.

SUZANNE: I don't believe that.

JOHN: It's true, believe me. I'd have married . . . anybody . . . I was lonely.

SUZANNE: I know. I've been like that since my husband died. Do you farm?

JOHN: Yes. I'm a farmer.

51

SUZANNE: Have you got a girlfriend?

JOHN: No.

SUZANNE: Was there ever anybody . . . important?

JOHN: No. Not for want of effort on my part I assure you.

SUZANNE: Your friend seems to have a way with girls.

JOHN: It was he who talked me into coming to the Show. I wouldn't have had the courage to come on my own. I'm lucky I suppose to have him. I wouldn't be here now talking to you if it hadn't been for him. At least I owe him that much.

SUZANNE: I'm obliged to Trudy in the same way. There I was sitting by the fire bemoaning my sad fate when she breezed in and announced that we were both going to the Spring Show. I jumped at the chance.

JOHN: Any family?

SUZANNE: Two daughters, both married with young families. I don't fit in. I like the kids but they start to annoy me after a while. I don't seem to have the patience for children any more. When your husband dies you're cut off. It's as simple as that. But here I am talking about myself all the time. What about you? Were you ever in love?

JOHN: You'll laugh if I tell you.

SUZANNE: The last thing I'll do is laugh. Were you?

JOHN: Several times. No. A hundred times. It never came to anything. I never even made love. I shouldn't have said that.

SUZANNE: Why not?

JOHN: I hardly know you.

SUZANNE: You did say you never made love?

JOHN: Yes.

SUZANNE: Why not?

JOHN: There were times when I thought it was a sin and other times when it just didn't work out. It never does, not for me.

SUZANNE: I can't believe it.

JOHN: It's true. What an admission to have to make at

52

my age. You'll think there's something wrong with me. I often think so myself. I've generally managed to mess up every relationship I ever had with a woman. I don't know how the hell I'm going to finish up.

SUZANNE: Come on, cheer up Johnny.

JOHN: And that's another thing —

SUZANNE: What?

JOHN: My name's not Johnny. Sylvester invented that. I suppose he thought it sounded sporty. John's my name, John.

SUZANNE: Very well I'll call you John. *(Puts her hand on his)* Come on, let's walk. It'll take our minds off our troubles.

JOHN: What about the others?

SUZANNE: I think Trudy will enjoy Sylvester's company better than mine.

JOHN: And you?

SUZANNE: You must have more confidence in yourself, John. Come on. *(They drift arm-in-arm across the stage. Volume of music increases)*

CURTAIN

* * * * *

LINK: *(They walk front).*

JOHN: I didn't know what she was getting at when she said I should have more confidence in myself. It's a terrible thing when you don't know if a woman is giving you a hint or not. Anyway we walked along and she put her arm in mine and it seemed the most natural thing in the world. Now and then she caught me looking at her and she smiled. We spent the evening together and then I brought her to her hotel. We stood in the foyer and I didn't know what to say.

* * * * *

ACT 2   SCENE 2

Action takes place in a hotel bedroom.

SUZANNE: Would you like a drink?

JOHN: Please.

SUZANNE: It's quiet in my room. We'll have it there. *(They move into bedroom where she starts to pour drinks)* Irish isn't it?

JOHN: Please. *(She pours drink)* I wonder where the others are?

SUZANNE: They're old enough to look after themselves. Are you worried?

JOHN: Good God no. *(She hands him drink)*

SUZANNE: Let's drink to the future.

JOHN: To the future. *(They quaff)*

SUZANNE: Do you dance?

JOHN: I move my legs. I doubt if you'd call it dancing.

SUZANNE: You're light on your feet. You should be good on a dance floor.
(She turns on radio. Immediately a blast of modern pop music assails their ears)

SUZANNE: Hardly suitable for us.
(She fiddles with dial until she finds a station from which drowsy, old-time dance music can be heard, possibly the September Song *or such. She takes his glass)*

SUZANNE: Let's dance.
(She deposits glasses)

JOHN: I'll try.
(Slowly they dance to the music, she humming the melody, John still a little bewildered)

SUZANNE: Relax John. There's nobody here but ourselves.
(Slowly they dance round the room. She stops and takes his hands)

SUZANNE: There's nothing to worry about.
(They dance again, this time cheek to cheek. They

54

come to where drinks are. She hands him his glass, takes her own. They drink, their heads close together. She kisses him)

SUZANNE: You finish your drink. I'll go and . . . change. *(She takes coat from bed and places it across a chair. She takes negligée from underneath pillow)* Unless you don't want to.

JOHN: I want to.

SUZANNE: I won't be long. Be ready for me. *(Exit)*

JOHN: *(To himself)* Be ready for her . . .
(Suitable music playing. He takes off his shortcoat and folds it slowly and carefully. He then takes off his shoes and stockings which he places near shortcoat. He takes off tie and shirt. He casts it aside. He takes off trousers to reveal a pair of shorts underneath. He casts trousers aside with abandon. Is about to shed shorts when suddenly he notices two figures standing each on a dais in a corner of room. They are spot-lighted. They are the brown-robed missionaries who used to come to Tubberganban)

JOHN: Oh no. Not you two. Go away for God's sake. Why are you always haunting me?
(One of the missionaries i.e. the cross missioner is abrasive and loud and allows himself to be carried away. The other i.e. the quiet missioner is gentle and forbearing, never raising his voice)

GENTLE M: Ye shall be chaste above all things and ye shall be modest in dress. Ye shall not scandalise the purity of womanhood.

JOHN: Oh God almighty what am I to do?

CROSS M: There was this man, this lecher. In the tavern he plied this woman with drink upon drink. Then he took the hapless creature to his hotel room and there he had his pleasure, his lustful animal pleasure. That night as he lay in his bed alone a sudden spasm seized him. In a moment he lay dead, dead, dead while his blackened soul sped to hell, yes, my dear brethren, straight to hell.

55

(Missioners disappear into darkness. John gropes for his trousers. Suddenly Suzanne appears in pink negligée)

SUZANNE: What's wrong John?

JOHN: *(Distressed)* Nothing.

SUZANNE: Come here John. It's alright John. Believe me it's alright. *(She takes his hands again)* You're not nervous now are you? *(John shakes his head)* You want me don't you? *(John nods his head)* Then kiss me.

(They kiss urgently and embrace. They kiss and caress seriously. Suddenly there is a deafening banging on the door. John is jolted backwards by the shock. The banging is repeated. John backs warily away from the door)

SUZANNE: Who is it?

VOICE: Open the door. Open at once.

SUZANNE: But who is it?

(Deafening knocking again. Fearfully Suzanne opens the door. Enter a young uniformed porter. There is a considerable commotion in the corridor outside)

SUZANNE: In God's name what's happening?

PORTER: *(Extends arms)* Come on get out of here. There's a bomb due to go off in three minutes.

SUZANNE: *(Screams)* A bomb. Oh God. A bomb. *(Screaming she runs into corridor)*

PORTER: Hurry sir. It's due to go off any minute.

JOHN: My pants. *(John gathers clothes round room)*

PORTER: There's no time. *(Pushes him)* In God's name get out of here. We're the last two in the building. *(Protesting John allows himself to be rushed out)*

CURTAIN

*   *   *   *   *

LINK: *(John comes downstage wrapped in a sheet and clutching his clothes. As he speaks he dresses)*

JOHN: Well may you laugh. Go on. I'm getting used to it. God almighty what a disaster. Everything going

56

so well and some eejit thinks it's a good joke to ring the hotel and say there's a bomb in the Ladies. A hoax — what would you expect with my luck. I hadn't even the satisfaction of seeing the whole bloody place blown up and myself along with it maybe. And what about Suzanne? She refused to have anything to do with me afterwards. I sent flowers to the hospital. I called several times. I met her doctor. He said it would be months before she got over the shock. Even then, he said, the sight of me would probably trigger it off again. She thinks I'm an I.R.A. bomber. And then Sylvester turned up again with another proposition.

CURTAIN

* * * * *

ACT 2   SCENE 3

John moves to kitchen. Simultaneously Eva shows in Sylvester.

EVA: Mister Brady Mister McLaine.
(With both hands Sylvester squeezes her waist from behind. She jumps forward surprised)
SILVESTER: How many times must I tell you to call me Sylvie . . . Now say it. Say Sylvie. Come on. Say Sylvie, say it.
EVA: Sylvie.
SILVESTER: Alright you can go about your business. There won't be any sandwiches tonight.
(Exit Eva)
JOHN: Where do you get your power over women?
SILVESTER: Long practice my friend.
JOHN: Alright. Tell us what brought you this hour of

57

the night?

SILVESTER: Pour me a drop of that brew and I'll come to the point.

(John locates glass and pours from ewer. Hands glass to Sylvester).

SILVESTER: You've heard oul' Brewer has passed on.

JOHN: The bookmaker?

SILVESTER: The very one.

SILVESTER: What has Brewer's death to do with your visit here?

SILVESTER: I have a proposition for you.

JOHN: *(Warily)* You have.

SILVESTER: With Brewer gone there's a vacancy for a bookie's shop in Bannabeen. I can muster two thousand if you put up two more. We'd be partners. After expenses we'd divide the profits down the line. What do you say?

JOHN: Two thousand is a lot. It's not my line of business. . .

SILVESTER: Let the business side of it to me. We can't go wrong. Just give me your cheque for two thousand and I'll have a solicitor draw up the agreement.

JOHN: Hold it. Hold it. I have no notion of forking out two thousand pounds.

SILVESTER: You want her? *(Points thumb towards where Eva has exited)*

JOHN: Who?

SILVESTER: Her. Eva. You want her?

JOHN: Are you trying to make an eejit out of me?

SILVESTER: Have I ever failed to produce the goods for you? Have I?

JOHN: No, but . . .

SILVESTER: It wasn't my fault if you missed the open goal. Would you have her if I got her for you?

JOHN: Of course.

SILVESTER: That's all I wanted to know. I have this damsel taped. Believe me when she's broken down there's nothing will satisfy her. Can't you see it man, the two of you sitting here watching telly across the winter. The wind howls outside. She fills your glass and her own. She sits on your lap and runs her fingers round the back of your neck. Your pulse quickens. Your heart misses a beat. She bites the bone behind your ear, a savage passionate bite. She drags you to her bedroom. I envy you, I really do.

JOHN: When will you ask her?

SILVESTER: What's wrong with right now, this very minute?

JOHN: You think she'll listen?

SILVESTER: Are you coming into partnership with me?

JOHN: I suppose so.

SILVESTER: Supposing is no good to me. Are you or aren't you?

JOHN: You'll have to give me time to think.

SILVESTER: No time. I must know now.

JOHN: All right.

SILVESTER: Good. You make tracks for the pub. Give me an hour alone with her and I'll lay the foundations. It won't be easy but I guarantee you your money's worth before the month is out. Now get out of here and let me to it.

JOHN: All right . . . you won't . . .

SILVESTER: I won't what?

JOHN: Forget yourself and put your own interests before mine?

SILVESTER: My plate is already full. You should know that. Now will you get out of here and let me get down to business.

JOHN: Goodnight and good luck. *(To audience)* Of course I shouldn't have gone. I should have known better than to trust a townie.

(Exit John. When Sylvester makes certain he has indeed gone he replenishes his glass and indulges in a wholesome swallow. He then whistles briefly, sonorously and a little imperiously. Sips as he waits.

59

Repeats whistle confidently. Eva emerges and advances coyly. Sylvester pours a dollup from ewer and hands it to her).

EVA: Where did he take off to at this hour?

SILVESTER: The pub.

EVA: Why didn't you go?

SILVESTER: Because I promised I'd speak on his behalf.

EVA: He's a manky little runt alright.

SILVESTER: I told him I'd put in a good word for him.

EVA: Don't make me laugh.

SILVESTER: You can pretend can't you?

EVA: Why should I?

SILVESTER: *(Puts his glass aside)* Come here, slut. *(Firmly)* I said come here.
(He flings his arms around her and kisses her expertly. They recoil when they've both had enough)

SILVESTER: You'll be nice to your man. You lead him on. Dangle your commodities in front of him. Be so near and yet so far and we'll be sitting pretty very soon.

EVA: You take a lot for granted don't you?

SILVESTER: Do I?

EVA: Yes you do. Whistling for me as if I were a bitch.

SILVESTER: You came didn't you? *(Tips her under chin)* Come on. Don't be coy with me. Or maybe you want to spend the rest of your life in this wilderness.

EVA: I'm only here to put by enough for a passage to Canada.

SILVESTER: That makes two of us. I have to get out. I've debts all over the place. You play your cards right and we'll be in Canada the end of the month.

EVA: You expect me to go off with you out of the blue. You have a neck you have.

SILVESTER: Why don't you just shut that sexy mouth of yours and come here. *(Firmly)* Come here.
(They kiss. They embrace. Lights out. End of scene)

CURTAIN

ACT 2   SCENE 4

The confessional at Tubberganban. A few weeks later. No array at either side this time. John at one side of confessional, elderly penitent at other. Father Kimmerley dismisses this person and turns his attention to John.

JOHN: I am not here for confession Father.

KIMMERLEY: Then would you mind leaving the box so that the others might be heard.

JOHN: There are no others. I waited till they had all gone.

KIMMERLEY: Why are you here?

JOHN: I have a notion Father of entering Holy Orders.

KIMMERLEY: *(Peers)* Who have I? Don't tell me. Let me guess. It's John Bosco McLaine isn't it?

JOHN: Correct.

KIMMERLEY: Now would you mind repeating yourself?

JOHN: I said I have a notion of entering Holy Orders.

KIMMERLEY: So long as it remains a notion we have nothing to worry about.

JOHN: I didn't expect you to be facetious.

KIMMERLEY: Sorry. Sorry. Sorry. Unintended I assure you. You see my son I am a product of Salamanca who was case-hardened in the slums of Pittsburg. The net result is that I have been turned into something of a sceptic. What precisely have you in mind?

JOHN: The Franciscans.

KIMMERLEY: There is no accounting for taste. Ah well I suppose it takes all kinds to make a world. If we hadn't Franciscans I daresay we'd have some other gaggle in their stead. So you want to be a priest. What age are you?

JOHN: I'll be fifty-three in July.

KIMMERLEY: And what self-respecting seminary is going to take you at that age?

JOHN: I don't expect any problem in that respect.

KIMMERLEY: Oh so you just walk in with your hat in your hand and walk out a priest after a few years. Well let me tell you something. Without a reference from me nobody will accept you.

JOHN: Does that mean you are withholding a reference?

KIMMERLEY: It does not. I'll tell you what I'll do. You come back here in three months time and if you're still serious I'll write and find out the Franciscan position regarding chaps like yourself. I'll say that as far as I know you're sound in wind and limb and have no history of mental disorder. Sure you're nearly halfway there already.

JOHN: What do you mean?

KIMMERLEY: Being a chastitute is first-class preparation for celibacy.

JOHN: I can do without sarcasm.

KIMMERLEY: I am not being sarcastic.

JOHN: You're opposed to my becoming a priest?

KIMMERLEY: Not quite.

JOHN: You think I'm doing the wrong thing?

KIMMERLEY: When all fruit fails we must try haws mustn't we?

JOHN: I'm at a loss to understand you Father.

KIMMERLEY: Let me ask you a question McLaine. Would certain recent events have anything to do with your decision?

JOHN: What events?

KIMMERLEY: Come now the whole parish knows that your housekeeper vanished suddenly. So also did Sylvester Brady. You weren't seen sober for a week after it.

JOHN: Do I get a reference?

KIMMERLEY: Come back in a month.

JOHN: A month will be too late.

KIMMERLEY: As far as I can see you want to be a priest overnight.

JOHN: And as far as I can see the only consolation for

me is to go back on the booze. There's no help for me here. *(Exit John)*

KIMMERLEY: John, John, come back . . .

CURTAIN

*   *   *   *   *

LINK: JOHN: *(Appearing with a bottle of whiskey)* There are times when the only thing to do is to booze it out. Drink till you're stupified. Sleep and try to escape. Wake up and it's all still there in front of you. More booze until you're exhausted. Then crawl back home . . . And God almighty what's the first sound you hear when you open the door . . .

*   *   *   *   *

ACT 2   SCENE 5

We hear the sound of the rosary as the lights come up on the kitchen. Praying are Father Kimmerley, Aunt Jane and Mickey. Enter John. The prayers stop and Aunt Jane rushes to him.

JANE: Oh John, John. God be thanked you're safe.

MICKEY: Good on you boy. I knew you'd wander in some night like this.

JOHN: Take it easy. I'm all right.

MICKEY: Sit down man. Sit down.

JANE: Two weeks John and no word. I thought something terrible had happened to you.

MICKEY: He was on the bottle ma'am. His bitterness had to run its course. Isn't that the way of it?

JOHN: That's the way of it.

KIMMERLEY: It's good to see you John.

JOHN: Thanks Father.

63

KIMMERLEY: I feel guilty about you. You came to talk about your troubles and I didn't take you seriously. I'm sorry.

JOHN: It wouldn't have made any difference Father. I know that, and you know it too. You know where the fault is.

KIMMERLEY: Yes I know where the fault is, it's in every catechism in this country. And I know *what* the fault is — the fault is that men like you, John, take sex far too seriously.

JANE: What a thing to say Father.

KIMMERLEY: It's true Miss McLaine, unfortunately.

MICKEY: I'm with you all the way Father. Some takes it so seriously it has them driven off their heads.

KIMMERLEY: It has us all driven off our heads, including myself.

JANE: Father?

KIMMERLEY: It's all right Miss McLaine, I have the protection of the years if not my collar.

JANE: I don't think I quite follow you Father.

KIMMERLEY: I'm sure you don't ma'am. But if you sat in the confessional like I do you'd wonder if marital sex or single chastity caused the most trouble. Men complaining their wives are frigid, women complaining their husbands want to make prostitutes of them, and bachelors like your nephew here devouring booze to stifle the nature rising up in them.

JANE: Merciful God those are terrible words for a priest to utter. We must do as the Church teaches.

KIMMERLEY: That is a matter of opinion. Oh have no doubt I uphold the teachings of the Church — but my sympathy is with those who suffer.

JANE: If we allow our animal passions to get the better of us where will it all end?

KIMMERLEY: *(Angrily)* I'm not talking abut animal passions Miss McLaine. I'm talking about sex.

MICKEY: Nature must have its fling ma'am if the world is to wheel free. Isn't that it Father?

KIMMERLEY: That's another way of putting it Mickey. I'll go now before I say too much . . . Goodnight John, I'll leave you in good hands.

JOHN: Goodnight Father.

JANE: I'll see you out Father.

KIMMERLEY: *(At door)* I'll pray for him Miss McLaine.

JANE: We'll all pray for him Father.

KIMMERLEY: Yes. At least we owe him that much . . . unless you have a better idea Mickey? *(Exit with Aunt Jane)*

(John takes glass and Mickey fills from ewer)

MICKEY: Everything will be fine from now on John. Your purgatory is behind you and there are joyful times ahead.

JOHN: Not for me there aren't.

MICKEY: Forget what happened. God never closed one door but he opened another.

JOHN: He slammed them in my face Mickey.

MICKEY: Not at all. *(Pauses)* Our friends Sylvie is gone.

JOHN: Good riddance.

MICKEY: Gone for good and glory and left a door open behind him. And left who standing there? I'll tell you who. Juleen McCoon from Tubbernaroon. *(John looks at him)* She'll be at the Crossroads dance Sunday night the same as always but this time she'll be a filly without a hobble, a filly waiting for a winkers, a filly waiting you might say to be nobbled by the right man. Or maybe you'd rather rest up awhile?

JOHN: *(Sits upright)* No. No. I'll be all right. I'll be all right. I'll give it one more fling and that will be my last.

MICKEY: You can't beat the old war-horse. All he wants is the smell of the powder and he's away into the thick of the fight. Drink up John. Drink up to Sunday night and to Juleen McCoon. *(They quaff)*

CURTAIN

* * * * *

LINK: JOHN: *(Coming forward)* You'd think I'd have learned from past misfortunes, but no. The love buds quicken and the sap flows once more. Never say die, that's my motto. And so I gird myself once more for the ouslaught. Once more to the Crossroads hopeful dance, there to sojourn and take my final chance.

* * * * *

ACT 2   SCENE 6

He enters the Crossroads pub, followed by Mickey. The usual patrons are present. The one-man band plays a tango merrily. All present dance and sing at the same time. Juleen McCoon stands near the band, cigarette in mouth, with her hands folded, tapping a foot to the beat of the tango. Mickey and John stand surveying the passing scene. Juleen lifts a hand and waves it at John. He checks to see if it's really he who is being saluted. He returns salute tentatively.

MICKEY: Go on man. You're in business. She's aiming herself at you. You'd have to be blind not to notice. Go on.

JOHN: You prophesied correctly. She's here and she seems willing.

MICKEY: There's no obstacle in your way tonight. Off you go, she won't wait forever. *(John goes hesitantly. Juleen joins him sultrily. She sweeps him off his feet and dances him around. The music stops. They come back to the table)*

MICKEY: Well now it must be said, because it would be a shame not to say it. I never saw such a well-matched couple on a dance floor. 'Tis like ye were

66

made for one another.

JULEEN: He brings out the best in me.

JOHN: It's the other way around. I couldn't dance to keep myself warm.

JULEEN: You're too modest. That's what's wrong with you.

MICKEY: Sit and I'll get you a drink. A whiskey for you John. And what about yourself Miss?

JULEEN: I'll take the same as Johnny here.

(Juleen gently pushes John onto chair, then sits on his lap. She takes his glass and holds it to his mouth. He sips, she sips)

JULEEN: Are you comfortable?

JOHN: Oh yes.

JULEEN: Am I too heavy for you?

JOHN: Oh God no.

JULEEN: Are you sure? *(Mickey returns with drinks)*

MICKEY: He was never so sure of anything in his life. Were you John?

JOHN: True Mickey, true. Never so sure. *(The music starts. Juleen jumps to her feet as the strains of a tango are heard)*

JULEEN: Come on Johnny . . . I hate to miss a dance. You won't be exhausted will you?

MICKEY: Look at him, if there's anyone exhausted before this night's out it'll be yourself girl. *(They dance. Mickey is delighted)*

ONE-MAN BAND: Thank you ladies and gentlemen. The next dance will be a ladies' choice. Please take your partners for a tango.

(Appropriate tango music. Juleen and John lead the floor. They are followed by other couples. Juleen dances the lead, taking long steps, John vainly tries to keep in touch. Suddenly a Travolta-like townie enters. He is followed by two thuggish satellites. He takes his cigarette from his mouth, tops it and places butt in lower inside coat pocket. He bears down on John and Juleen. He taps John on shoulder. John

67

turns round)

TOWNIE: Excuse me.

(He takes Juleen in his arms and sweeps her out of John's reach to the delight of his friends. John stands foolishly watching the dancing pair. They come his way. He taps townie on shoulder. Townie stops. Music stops)

TOWNIE: Yes?

JOHN: Excuse me.

(John goes about taking Juleen in his arms but he is firmly taken by the collar and pulled backwards by townie whose friends move menacingly forward)

JOHN: You excused me. I have the same right to excuse you.

TOWNIE: But it isn't an excuse-me. It's a ladies' choice.

JOHN: The lady happened to choose me.

TOWNIE: Is that so?

JOHN: Before you came in.

TOWNIE: Exactly. Before I came in. But now I'm in and you're out. The lady has chosen me.

JOHN: No she hasn't.

TOWNIE: Why don't you ask her?

JOHN: I'm not afraid of you Mister whoever you are.

TOWNIE: Ask the lady.

JOHN: Is it to be me or him?

JULEEN: Why don't you go home? There's nothing here for you.

JOHN: So that's the way is it. I should have known better.

(Townie gently pushes Juleen to one side. He raises his fists. John raises his. The two satellites move in from behind and beat John to the ground. He rises and is helped by Mickey whose help he spurns. He staggers out into the night. The dance resumes. Business as usual)

CURTAIN

ACT 2   SCENE 7

Action takes place in kitchen.

JOHN: Damn him. Damn the townie. Damn all townies. There should be a union in every parish in this country to keep out townies. Dammit, we country-men should be first served in the event of there being certain merchandise on the market, if you know what I mean. *(His imagination works)*
(Enter Sylvester and two girls. They circle him)

JOHN: Strong measures should be taken to control these bucks from towns and cities. They should be deprived of their vital organs and these should be transfixed on telegraph poles and piers of gates as a warning to all would-be seducers from outside the area.
(Behind him, the trio laugh, and exit up-stage)

JOHN: Go away. Go away. *(Shouts after them)* Go to hell.
(Enter two missioners)

CROSS M: Hell.

GENTLE M: Hell.

CROSS M: Hell.

JOHN: Oh God. Oh my God. You might say it all began with those two missioners. I'll never forget the way their robes billowed like sails when they scoured the parish for confession dodgers and assorted transgressors.
(As he talks Juleen and townie walk into view with arms around each other)

MISSIONERS: *(Sing)* Faith of our fathers holy faith,
We will be true to thee till death.
Oh how our hearts beat high with joy!

JOHN: My heart didn't beat high with joy. It beat high with terror at the thought of hell.

CROSS M: Are you prepared to roast in hell's fire for all eternity in exchange for one moment of animal passion?

JOHN: For pity's sake I never had one moment of animal passion. That's what has me the way I am.

CROSS M: There is no outrage more hateful to God, as when a man made in God's likeness lures an innocent girl along the road to damnation.

JOHN: If you think all young girls are innocent you're a fool.

CROSS M: Do you think God is a fool? Do you? Do you?

JOHN: No.

GENTLE M: *(Organ music)* Take your beads in your hands and repeat after me. I will be true to my Catholic faith. I will shun the society of those who lead me into evil ways. I will never sin with a woman.

JOHN: Shut up. Shut up. What right have you to dictate to me? Is Holy Ireland right and the rest of the world wrong? Why were me and my unfortunate equals chosen above other races to preserve our virginity as if it were a sacred relic? Why us? Why me?

ALL: Virgin most pure.

JOHN: You took away my dignity. Without my dignity I am nothing.

ALL: Virgin most chaste.

JOHN: You made me feel ashamed.

ALL: Tower of Ivory.

JOHN: A man can have a woman without shame almost anywhere on earth except in this insane place.

ALL: Refuge of sinners.
 Queen conceived without original sin.
 Queen of peace.
 (Women laugh at him)

JOHN: *(Takes gun)* Look at them. Look at them. They haunted me all my life — missioners, townies, women — most of all women. I'll never get away from them. Except one way. I'm going to blow my brains out while I still have some shred of dignity left, while I still resemble in some way the man I'm supposed to be. So here goes and they can say what they like about me when I'm gone. *(Raises gun)* No. I've a better idea! *(Fires, laughs)* Yes, I've a better idea. Why should I do it suddenly with a gun when this way is just as sure. *(Indicates punch)* It will take a bit longer but it's just as sure and who is to say whether it's a sin or not? It's not suicide. I'll fox them, by God I'll fox them. They don't know the crying loneliness of nights without end, the barrenness of summer days when all the world is singing, but me, that has no note left to join in. A toast! *(Lifts bottle)* To the end of loneliness and pain, and of John Bosco McLaine, who died for want of love.

CURTAIN